The Art of Putting

Paul Trevillion is a legendary British sports artist and the inventor of the Pencil Grip putting method. He holds a teaching diploma in Art and Design, and is noted as the cartoonist for the 'Roy of the Rovers' comic strip and as the brainchild behind the 'You are the Ref' series in the *Observer*. He is the author and illustrator of over twenty golf books, including *Gary Player's Golf Class*, which became the largest syndicated feature in the world, appearing in over 1500 newspapers. Now aged eighty-three, Paul Trevillion lives in the beautiful Hertfordshire countryside, just a four wood from a choice of golf courses, and he still never misses a four-foot putt.

D0682727

The Art of Putting

Trevillion's Method of Perfect Putting

PAUL TREVILLION

MICHAEL JOSEPH
an imprint of
PENGUIN BOOKS

MICHAEL JOSEPH

UK | USA | Canada | Ireland | Australia
India | New Zealand | South Africa

Michael Joseph is part of the Penguin Random House group of companies
whose addresses can be found at global.penguinrandomhouse.com.

Penguin
Random House
UK

First published in Great Britain as *Missing Impossible* by Pelham Books 1996
Reissued with new material 2017
001

Copyright © Paul Trevillion, 1996, 2017

The moral right of the author has been asserted

The original edition of this book was published as
The Perfect Putting Method by Paul Trevillion
by Pelham Books 1971

Set in 12/15 pt Garamond MT Std
Typeset by Jouve (UK), Milton Keynes
Printed in Great Britain by Clays Ltd, St Ives plc

A CIP catalogue record for this book is available from the British Library

ISBN: 978–0–718–18956–3

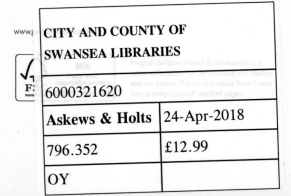

CITY AND COUNTY OF
SWANSEA LIBRARIES

6000321620

Askews & Holts	24-Apr-2018
796.352	£12.99
OY	

Contents

Part One

INTRODUCTION

In the year 1970 I rejected the traditional hands together putting grip. I took my left hand out of putting: I relied on my dominant right hand and was called a putter nutter.

In the year 1475 Michelangelo was born. Michelangelo took his left hand out of art: he relied on his dominant right hand and was called 'the divine one'.

Raffaello da Montelupo, who was a sculptor and architect of the Italian Renaissance, was also an apprentice to Michelangelo.

These are the words of Raffaello: 'Michelangelo was naturally left-handed, but always used his right hand in his art. As far as I know, Michelangelo never made anything with his left hand.'

Even those not interested in art are aware of the most influential artist in history, Michelangelo, a prolific sculptor, painter and architect, who painted the ceiling of the Sistine Chapel. He was also the chief architect who designed the vast dome and rebuilding of St Peter's Basilica in Rome.

How Michelangelo Found His Dominant Right Hand in Art

Michelangelo's inexhaustible thirst for knowledge in the field of anatomy inspired his decision to switch from being naturally left-handed to painting with his right hand.

Each hand is controlled by the opposite half of the brain.

Left hand to right side of brain – emotional, willing to take risks, sensitive to thoughts, asks 'why?' more often than 'how?'.

Right hand to left side of brain – logical, doesn't like to take risks, prefers things with concrete rules, asks 'how?' more often than 'why?'.

Uniform clarity of focus and a graceful classic line — these were the trademarks of Michelangelo the Master.

It was Michelangelo's dominant right hand that created so many of the most famous paintings in the history of art.

'If people knew how hard I worked to get my mastery, it wouldn't seem so wonderful at all' – Michelangelo.

Chapter 1

The Pencil Grip

In 1970 I decided to reject the traditional hands-together putting grip. I parted my hands and in doing so I took my left hand out of the putting stroke. I now relied on my dominant right hand. By holding the putter in the same way I held a pencil I discovered a uniform clarity of focus. I could draw a perfectly straight line when taking the putter back and through. Also the putter face remained square to the hole throughout the putting stroke.

The position of the bottom hand, holding the putter shaft like a pencil, ensures the wrist does not turn during the stroke.

I was determined to create that same confident feel of drawing with a pencil in my studio when out on the green putting with my Pencil Grip. I made a decision: draw then putt.

I spent thirty minutes in my studio working on a portrait of Jack Nicklaus. Then, holding the putter with the same Pencil Grip, I spent thirty minutes on the putting mat holing four-foot putts. I returned to finish the Jack Nicklaus portrait.

Jack Nicklaus

It took several days drawing and putting before I felt as confident when holding a putter as I did holding a pencil. I even attached a pencil to the putter face and then checked the line back and through with the putter. It was ruler straight.

I had long gone past the days when I hoped a four-foot putt would drop. The Pencil Grip was infallible. From the moment the ball left the putter face it had nowhere to go but into the hole.

From four feet there is no borrow on any green that dictates the putt. With the Pencil Grip the ball, if struck firmly enough, will eliminate any borrow and the putt will drop.

It was a man from Pretoria, South Africa, Branden Grace, who surpassed all my Pencil Grip expectations in a major championship.

At The Open on Saturday 22 July 2017, played at Royal Birkdale, Branden Grace made golfing history as the first man to shoot 62 in a major championship. Ben Hogan, Arnold Palmer, Jack Nicklaus, Gary Player, Nick Faldo and Tiger Woods – golfing legends – never reached that magical figure.

Branden Grace

Branden Grace completed his eight under par round of 62 using the Pencil Grip, finally achieving what so many players had failed to do because golfing history had proved far too big a barrier to overcome.

Bernhard Langer

The Claw Grip

At the British Senior Open 2017, Royal Porthcawl, fifty-nine-year-old Bernhard Langer claimed a record tenth Senior major putting with his hands apart, employing the Broom Handle with the Claw Grip.

It was one more Senior major than Gary Player achieved, and he did it by defying the views of the putting experts of yesteryear.

It was not the first time he had done so: Langer also had success in the majors with the Trevillion Split Hand Mirror Grip putting stroke.

Chapter 2
The Traditional Golf Putting Grip

In highly tense situations, such as a crucial putt on the 18th green to win a major, even hardened professionals can 'choke', because the added pressure makes them aware that their trusted traditional putting grip on such occasions has previously let them down.

There is no better example than Tom Watson on the 18th green at Turnberry in the 2009 Open. Leading the tournament by one shot, Watson, fifty-nine years old and using a traditional putting grip, had the golden opportunity to make history as the oldest major winner.

Watson's tee shot found the middle of the fairway. The eight-iron approach landed on the green, but ran on into the fringe, stopping at the thick grass.

Watson decided against chipping back on to the green. Instead he hit the putt far too hard and it ended up eight feet past the hole. Watson missed the return putt to record a bogey and was then beaten in a play-off by Stewart Cink.

The crucial return eight-foot putt that Watson needed to win The Open was never going to drop. Watson admits,

Tom Watson's traditional putting grip

'I know what I did wrong. I blocked it with my left hand going through.'

I believe the left hand in the traditional putting grip is one of the main reasons why so many sinkable putts are missed in tense situations.

Success or failure in both art and golf is entirely dependent on the left hand. As already noted, each of our hands is connected to the opposite side of the brain.

The left hand to the right side of the brain – automatic behaviour.

The right hand to the left side of the brain – conscious movement.

The fact that the left hand relies on automatic behaviour means that you are not always fully focused and in full control of it; this can be a destructive combination when putting.

Chapter 3

The Connection Between Art and Golf

In art, as in golf, the hands create what only the eyes can see.

'I saw the angel in the marble and carved until I set it free' – Michelangelo.

Michelangelo's *David* by Trevillion

As an artist, I have never seen a piece of white paper. There is always an image of some description on it that only I can see. Then with the pencil, I draw the image and everyone can see it.

A similar principle applies to golf. Only the golfer on the tee can see the area of the fairway in which he intends the ball to land. Then he strikes the ball and the gallery, providing the ball was struck accurately, see it land on the area of the fairway the golfer had envisioned on the tee.

Both painting and putting are impossible without additional equipment:

Take the pencil out of the hand of the artist – no drawing.

Take the putter out of the hand of the golfer – no dropped putt.

No artist can claim to have painted a canvas. It was the brush that placed the paint.

No golfer can claim to have sunk a putt. It was the putter face that holed the ball.

This is why painting is so difficult and putting at times almost impossible. It requires controlling the brush or the putter with your hands.

This is different from other sports.

It was the hand of Michael Jordan that dropped the basketball into the basket.

It was the fist of Muhammad Ali that landed for the KO punch.

It was the foot or head of Pele that sent the ball into the net.

Michael Jordan

So we have to accept that even golf's 'Big Three' – Palmer, Nicklaus and Player – never holed out. It was the putter face that struck the ball.

Having said that, all three when the putter was in their hands were magicians on the green. This was the reason why Palmer, Nicklaus and Player won 34 majors between them. They had the mental toughness to strike the ball firmly with the putter face, getting it rolling forward, hugging the green, and invariably the ball disappeared below ground.

Chapter 4

Putting – A Right-Handed Game

As long as we live we will never find a hole that will come and meet the ball; the ball must go to the hole.

Unless you make more than your share of long putts, you are never going to win many tournaments. The greatest putter I have had the pleasure to see on the greens was the young Tiger Woods, who always went for the hole. No golfer in history sank as many long putts to win majors as Tiger Woods. It seemed every time Tiger lined up a putt it would disappear into the hole.

Tiger believes that putting is a right-handed game. He is right. And to my mind there has never been an equal to the young Tiger Woods on the green.

Woods reminded me of Palmer in his major-winning days: he also went for the hole. Even if Palmer knocked the ball four feet past, the return was a gimmee. Unfortunately his success didn't last, and this has also been the case with Tiger Woods.

No artist has ever pushed a pencil when drawing, and no golfer will ever make a good putt by pushing the ball.

Tiger Woods

In tense situations when facing a crucial sinkable putt, golfers are too often guilty of pushing instead of striking through the ball. The result: another missed putt.

Chapter 5

Perspective Means Perfection on the Greens

It was the Renaissance artist Paolo Uccello, born in 1397, who pioneered perspective, opening the door for other artists to follow.

When I left college in 1952 I started working as a designer for Laszlo Hoenig in Mayfair, London. Laszlo Hoenig was one of the world's leading interior designers and in his studio I learned the art of perspective. I designed interiors for hotels, offices and studios, and it was how I used the lines of perspective that made the space available look very large or very small.

Professional golfers before they go out to compete learn to a reasonable degree, out on the practice putting green, the pace of the roll of the ball. They learn even more after they have played the first two or three holes.

So why do golfers sometimes leave a very long putt four feet short, knock it four feet past or even five feet to the side of the hole?

In many cases, possibly in most cases, golfers have limited knowledge of perspective on the greens. They are easily deceived by the shapes, slopes and contours and misread the length of the putt.

I have never professed to be a golfer. I am an artist. But because of my knowledge of perspective I can read greens. I am never fooled by borrows, slopes or irregular sizes.

Try the simple tests on the following pages and see how many you get right. You will then know how expertly your eyes read the perspective when checking out the borrows and slopes on the green.

Perspective I

Which line to the hole looks longer?

*Get your measuring stick out, then check each line.
You will find both lines are the same length.*

It is a two-level green. Which is the larger area, top or bottom?

Both greens are exactly the same size.

Green slopes up towards the hole.

Green slopes down away from the hole. Which line on the two greens is longer?

Both lines on the greens are exactly the same length.

One Point Perspective

I believe a little knowledge of perspective can increase the number of putts the golfer drops during a round by at least two. On short putts, when looking from ball to hole, the golfer needs only a single perspective. One Point Perspective identifies how lines that travel away from the golfer recede in the distance.

Check this out for yourself when looking down a very long, straight road. As the sides of the road get further away, they appear to get closer together and finally diminish towards a single point far ahead of you. That is One Point Perspective.

Golfers, on short putts of four feet or under, who study the contours of the green and check the putt from every conceivable angle only create points of confusion that interfere with a straightforward putt. On four-foot putts, I stand behind the ball and look from ball to hole, thus utilizing One Point Perspective. Then I simply knock the ball in. Another putt sunk.

Take a pin to represent a golf flag, stick it in a piece of paper and draw four straight lines of equal length at varying angles. Although it does not appear so to the naked eye, you know that all four lines are the same size. Knowledge of One Point Perspective will keep you from being fooled.

Chapter 6

An Artist's Secret for Holing Short Putts

An artist draws what he sees, guided by what he *knows*.

In my drawing of Rory McIlroy, I was guided by what I *know* from my anatomy studies as to the position of the unseen hands behind his head holding the golf club. I was thus able to determine the correct line of the golf club shaft at the end of McIlroy's swing.

On short putts I never see the hole reduced by perspective to an eclipse.

I see what I *know*, which is the golf hole from a *birds eye view*.

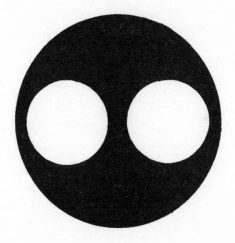

More than large enough to swallow *two* golf balls.

The daunting target of a golf ball hole becomes a much larger one when visualized from above. This is the reason why I never feel any pressure and never miss a four-foot putt.

Part Two

THE MECHANICS OF THE METHOD

Chapter 7

The Four-Foot Miss that Changed My Life

Let's start at the very beginning. The year 1968 and the four-foot miss that changed my life.

It was a simple, no borrow, four-foot putt. All I had to do for an eagle was knock the ball in the hole. I can recall now how I set myself over the putt and stroked the ball towards the hole. It was on line and dead centre of the hole. But as I straightened up I knew it wasn't going to drop, and it didn't. It stopped a good three inches short. For a moment I stood there looking at it; I was so annoyed I was numb. A few minutes earlier I had just hit two perfect golf shots – the first a drive of a little over 200 yards which had comfortably cleared the river on the par-5 15th at Enfield Golf Club. The ball came to rest in the middle of the fairway, I was able to take a three wood for my second shot. I hit the ball well. It sailed over the hill where, to my joy, it rolled down over the dry hard fairway and on to the green, coming to rest no more than four feet from the hole. Having never reached this green in two before I was, for the first time, putting for an eagle.

There was no way I could miss the putt – but I did. How? Even today I still do not know.

Having missed, I decided not to putt out for a 4. I simply walked up and knocked the ball off the green. In my anger I hit the ball hard, very hard, and it disappeared into some rough at the side of the green. I kept on walking, I didn't even bother to look for it. I climbed up on to the 16th tee and hit two consecutive drives into the out-of-bounds on the right. They proved to be the last two golf shots to be hit by me on a golf course for over a year. I rammed my driver deep into the golf bag and stormed off.

On the drive home I replayed the putt a dozen times and, of course, the ball always dropped – but what was the point? In two strokes I had covered, to perfection, 453 yards only to be cheated by the last four feet. It seemed so pointless that so much good play could be undone by a few miserable feet on the green. It was no comfort admitting that everybody misses their share of short putts – why should they? Ask yourself, what would a professional do if, from the tee, he hit only a handful of fairways during a round? The answer is obvious, he would take his swing to pieces. Yet I have seen golfers – professional golfers – take 35–40 putts a round, failing to register a single one-putt green because they missed from within the four-foot mark more times than I guess they would care to admit. And yet, strangely enough, they accept it, assured by the thought that the putts will drop tomorrow – but, of course, as we all know, they never do. And yet these same golfers will, if they have missed two greens with their approach shots, go out and practise at length that department of their game.

Ask a professional why he is not out there on the putting green endeavouring to perfect his putting stroke and he will, as likely as not, tell you: 'You've got to be a born putter. No amount of practising will make you one; it's all in the mind.' Truth is, that hot summer I believed the same. I had been missing more than my share of short putts. The fun had gone out of the game. Hell, if you can't sink the putts, what's the point of getting the ball on the green in the first place? So I decided to give up the game, and I did. I have never played a serious round of golf since.

Chapter 8

Joe Davis Shows the Way

Although I had stopped playing the game of golf, I couldn't stop thinking about it. Why should putting be so difficult, not only for myself but for every class of golfer? I refused to accept the theory that good putters are born. Such a doctrine didn't hold water. There was nothing difficult about knocking a ball along the ground, it required no special gifts of nature – a child could do it. No, nearer the truth was that golfers in general spent 90 per cent of their time practising the shots that were to get them on the green. Only a grudging 10 per cent was allocated to practising their putting. Little wonder that tournament professionals never completely master the simple art of putting.

Strange as it may seem, I was inspired to take out my putter again after watching the top snooker champions in action. Since that day in 1955 when Joe Davis registered his crowning achievement – snooker's maximum break of 147 (15 reds, 15 blacks and all the colours) – I had always taken a great interest in snooker. Possibly this is why I had never accepted the argument that putting brings about numerous mental pressures because of the time factor involved. Agreed, in football, tennis, rugby, etc., the mental pressures are slightly less, for here the ball, is played to you and you react instinctively. Nevertheless, in sports comparable to golf – snooker, archery and shooting, for example – one has to propel the object to the target from a stationary position, and it is very rare indeed for participants in one of these sports to suffer from the dreaded 'shakes' which for one reason or another attack many world-class golfers when they step on to the putting surface.

When watching Joe Davis play I always formed the opinion that it was a far tougher proposition to knock a snooker ball into the pocket from ten feet than it is to knock a perfectly straight putt in from four feet. I am sure you will agree that the mental pressures in all world-class sports are uniform, and yet I never once saw Joe Davis attempt to lag up when ten feet from the pocket. This, of course, is one of the secrets why snooker players and the like do not suffer from the 'yips'. Every time they line up the ball – and, remember, they sometimes have to knock it in off two cushions, every bit as difficult as negotiating a borrow on the green – they have a positive attitude.

They are concentrating on one thing: ball to pocket. Striving for perfection with every stroke teaches snooker players to live with and overcome pressure. This is why Arnold Palmer in his heyday was, by far, the best putter I had ever seen. He always went for the hole.

At all times, the snooker player, the archer, the shooter aim for perfection – they have to if they are to score well.

Arnold Palmer

Not so the golfer. The truth is, golf is a game that allows for too great a margin for error. Only on the putting green do golfers strive for absolute perfection. Possibly this is why it is only on the putting green that the pressure affects them.

From the tee a golfer can be as much as twenty feet off line and still reach the fairway. An approach shot can be twenty feet from the flag and still on the green. Both shots will receive generous applause from the gallery. A twenty-foot putt that lags two feet short will receive even greater applause. In no other sport can such a margin of error receive such high appraisal. A bowler at cricket need be no more than eight inches off line to miss the wicket. When batting, an error of judgement of as little as two inches will snick a possible catch. The prize fighter has to be no more than a sixteenth of an inch out to miss an opponent altogether.

Possibly a better example is the juggler on the stage – how many times have you seen one of these performers put a spoon on the toe of his shoe, flick it up eight feet in the air and land it in a cup balanced on his head? Jugglers can do this time after time because they have a positive thought action; they allow no margin for error. Unlike the golfer, the juggler has no thoughts of lagging up, the spoon must drop into the cup every time.

Here was the answer. Golfers, especially on the green, apply only part of their concentration to knocking the ball in the hole. The mechanics of the swing dominate their thoughts; at least 90 per cent of their concentration is applied to keeping their head and body still, taking the putter back square to the hole, accelerating through the ball and then following through square to the hole.

THE SNOOKER PLAYER CONCENTRATES ON WHERE HE IS GOING TO HIT THE BALL; THE GOLFER CONCENTRATES ON *HOW* HE IS GOING TO HIT IT.

I am quite sure I am right here, more so after seeing Joe Davis at a pro-am golf tournament. Davis, faced with a four-foot putt, lay full stretch on the green and knocked the ball in using the handle-end of the putter exactly like a cue. Two holes later he had another four-foot putt. I thought he was going to repeat his snooker act. Instead, he lined it up like a tournament professional, went through his pre-putting drill – and missed. Davis had fallen for the four-card trick.

The first stage of my new putting stroke was to split my hands on the club, the same way a snooker player splits his hands on the cue. A right-handed snooker player steadies the cue with his left hand and hits the ball with his right – thinking ball-to-pocket. I copied. I steadied the putter with the left hand, extended my right hand down the shaft, and concentrated on just knocking the ball into the hole, using my right hand only. I thought of only one thing – ball-to-hole. I practised this way with every length of putt from two feet to twenty feet. I was after perfection, and since that day I have never lagged a putt.

At first I found it hard to believe that every four-foot putt would drop but as the days passed I learned to accept my invincibility. I was infallible and two years later, in January 1970, I wrote about my findings in *Golf Illustrated*. By this time I had sunk countless thousands of four-foot putts without missing once. In that same period of time not one world-class golfer came within an ocean of my achievement ... Archer, Charles, Player, Palmer and Casper, all the world's great putters, had missed their share of four-footers during that time.

I claimed in print that I could beat them all and I issued a challenge to every golfer in the world. The stake – £1,000 upwards. The distance from the hole – four feet. I knew I could beat all-comers so I sat back and waited for the chance to prove it.

Chapter 9

The Challengers Came – We Putted –
I Conquered

My challenge did not go unheeded, letters poured into the *Golf Illustrated* offices, my telephone did not stop ringing, one man even travelled all the way down from Scotland with a £200 challenge. *Golf Illustrated* gave it front-page coverage and this is the story they carried on 29 January 1970:

The Putts Are Dropping!
Trevillion undefeated – wins £200 on one putt and gives it to charity.
Peter Willis reports
The signs indicate that the Trevillion putting method for four-footers and under, publicised in this magazine last week, will be seen in force on the golf courses this Spring. Initial reaction from club golfers who have tried the split-hand method is that it works!

Trevillion, who has now stepped up his daily practice to a minimum of 1,000 putts, has one problem – he has had to alter his routine of hitting a chair leg from four feet – the reason is obvious, the repeated striking is making the chair unstable!

As for the challengers, Trevillion (the world's No. 1 putter) as was expected received many from local golfers. On this Trevillion told me: 'They could certainly knock the putts in, but when the chips were down and they were putting for high stakes they missed.'

Still undefeated, Trevillion repeats his challenge of last week to play any golfer in the world, amateur or professional, over a series of four-foot pressure putts.

One challenger who has travelled all the way down from Scotland, knocked up Trevillion at his London home and issued a direct challenge.

Trevillion was entertaining friends at the time and the challenger, Mr Willie McCrae of Glasgow, refused an offer to putt on the carpet, he demanded natural conditions.

So Trevillion motored up to his home course, Enfield, where on the sixth green he won the challenge match and was £200 richer!

During the match which lasted two putts (Trevillion holed, McCrae missed) Trevillion inadvertently interrupted a member practising to the green. To this member Trevillion extends his apologies.

We would like now to make it plain that Trevillion is not prepared to accept any more direct challenges. In future those who dispute Trevillion's claim as the world's No. 1 putter must first file their challenge through the *Golf Illustrated* offices.

As yet no professional had accepted the challenge, I was merely beating local golfers. Very few could raise the initial £1,000 stake, although one did put up a Rover Automatic. Even now I can still remember his face when I drove away in it. About this time Tom Scott, the BBC golf broadcaster, christened me 'The Messiah'. This is what he wrote as editor of *Golf Illustrated*:

By this time readers will be well aware that our valued contributor, Paul Trevillion, is both outspoken and brave. Each of his articles produce a flood of letters, some for Trevillion and some against Trevillion, for it seems you either love him or hate him.

But his claim to be the world's best putter has brought out more letters than anything else he has ever written and I understand that somehow or other readers have found out his home address and telephone number, and have also contacted him there.

Alas, I have no claim to be the world's best putter although I fancied myself pretty good on the greens at one time, but some practising in the office would seem to indicate that he has something in his new putting method. But his main theme is that his putting ideas work when a golfer is under pressure and when the rewards are high.

And whether you believe in his theories or don't believe in them you must agree that his arguments are sound, and can't be dismissed just as the thinking of some fanatic.

It could be, therefore, that Trevillion is the new golf Messiah. He certainly gets to the root of things.

Not all agreed with what he said. Ryder Cup player Brian Huggett, for instance, had some unkind things to say in the same magazine.

Trevillion is talking a lot of rubbish when he claims that he is the world's greatest putter. I don't honestly believe he has sunk a pressure putt in his life. As for the Rover car he said he won I wouldn't like to comment on that.

He mentions Paul Runyan's method of putting with a split-handed grip. Well I played with Runyan and Snead in the 1962 Open at Troon — I finished third as a matter of fact — and in fairness Runyan holed a lot of good putts but he still missed some.

I much prefer the upright putters. People like Billy Casper, Peter Thomson and Peter Butler, who is really a fine pressure-putter.

But I must admit that Bonallack putts with his chin on the green. Archer also gets well down there which underlines that putting is a very individual game and it is the method which gets the ball into the hole I recommend using.

If it has got to be a change in style I would go for the Alliss method — right hand over left. I used it myself when an assistant. I was going through a pretty bad spell on the greens at the time.

I don't believe in such an exaggerated parting of the hands as Trevillion suggests. By splitting the hands you don't get the control that you do with, say for example, the Vardon grip.

Huggett's fellow Ryder Cup man Neil Coles showed more perception:

I don't find Trevillion's putting method particularly new, in fact if I remember rightly, David Snell won the Match-Play Championship with it in 1959. And then for some reason abandoned it.

I myself have never tried this, possibly because I don't think such a method would stand up against the techniques employed by such as Peter Thomson or Bobby Locke at their best.

The advantages of this method, and I'm speaking in the interest of club members who might, if in trouble, give it a try, are . . . it gets your eyes right over the ball and it gives plenty of leverage in the right hand.

Trevillion's anchor-point is the left hand which he positions at the top of the club. He uses his right to swing the club through pendulum-fashion.

If I really found trouble with my putting this season I might give it a try, but I would have to be in pretty desperate straits to do it.

Finally my views are that golf is an old game, full of theories, and it seems to me the one method which has stood the test of time is the upright one.

Coles had a point here, but this was the first time the upright method for putting had received a healthy challenger. At that moment I was convinced that not only would many golfers throughout the country change to my method, they would, what's more, win with it.

Chapter 10

I Lose My Amateur Status

The inevitable happened, the Royal and Ancient Golf Club, the ruling body of golf in Britain, informed me that I had forfeited my amateur status. The reason being that I was receiving payment for the method golf instruction I was writing in the magazine *Golf Illustrated*. My first reaction was to apply to the PGA for the necessary forms which would enable me to play the professional circuit full-time.

I did not, for one moment, imagine that I was going to win a tournament but here, I believed, was my chance to step on to a green with a well-known professional and outputt him, so proving my method was superior. I knew I could outputt every pro and now I intended to prove it in front of the golfing galleries.

Unfortunately the PGA put a stop to this; they came back and informed me that I did not have the necessary credentials to join their association. Like any other professional body, the PGA have certain rules and requirements before accepting entrants:

(1) I had to wait five years before becoming a full member of the PGA and I could only do this by qualifying at the official PGA training centre. In that five-year period I was not eligible to take part in PGA tournaments.

(2) Assistants to professionals can become full members within three years subject to qualifying at the training centre. They can then play in PGA tournaments six months after registering with the Association.

(3) To walk straight into the tournaments, as I had expected, I would, on application to the PGA, have had to have been of international standing as an amateur, recommended by the PGA Sectional Committee and be under twenty-five years of age. Six months after such an application, providing of course that I was accepted, I could have played in their tournaments.

I was now in a self-imposed golfing limbo – I could not play as an amateur, neither could I play as a professional. As a golfer, I did not exist – but the method did.

Ben Sayers, the oldest club manufacturers in the world, stepped on to the scene. It was their intention to produce an exact replica of the putter I, myself, employed. Mr P. W. Millard, their managing director, impressed me with his enthusiasm. I had no second thoughts about signing with his company. Sayers already had under contract the then reigning USPGA champion Ray Floyd and the colourful Doug Sanders. It was said in many quarters that with my signature Sayers now had golf's 'Big Three'.

I had spent a year working out the designs for the putter I used. It was centre-shafted with an all-leather grip which terminated approximately eight inches from the blade. The heavy brass head had a pencil sighting mark on the top. Its overall length – thirty inches. Sayers went into production immediately; it was to be called the 'Pencil Putter'.

Four weeks after signing with Ben Sayers I received a prototype Pencil Putter; three days later it was put to the test in a unique putting challenge match.

International showbiz star Adam Faith had just spent a five-hour session in my studio, where his old putting method had been stripped away to be replaced by my split-hand method. Previously he had hit rock-bottom at Ganton. There he drove the 17th only to three-putt; then he hit two tremendous shots at the 18th to make the green and then experienced the horror of four-putting. Those seven putts on those two holes, he told me, absolutely destroyed him. Before our meeting he was seriously considering giving up the game.

Armed with my method and the prototype Pencil Putter, Adam Faith went out and beat former Ryder Cup star Syd Scott in a tremendously exciting 18-hole impromptu challenge match at Roehampton Golf Club.

After his defeat, Syd Scott had this to say: 'On Adam Faith's efforts against me, the reports on the method have certainly not been exaggerated. When he missed a very short putt at the second I thought he had gone. It's a tribute to the method that he came back and won.'

On that short missed putt, Adam had this to say: 'I thought my ball was interfering with Syd's line so I asked

When you putt the
Trevillion way with the
Ben Sayers new
Pencil Putter.

The hole looks
much bigger.

This is Paul Trevillion demonstrating his
famous putting method using the new
Pencil Putter made specially by Ben Sayers.

If you're having scoring problems—and
let's face it who hasn't—try the
Sayers-Trevillion combination.

And in no time your putting problems
will look a whole lot smaller.

In fact there's a good chance they'll
disappear—

Into a great big hole.

Each putter is supplied with
instructional leaflet describing
this unique method.

BEN SAYERS North Berwick Scotland

The Ben Sayers advert that appeared in the golfing press

Adam Faith

him if he wanted me to mark it. He nodded and made a half waving gesture with his hand. Then the thought ran through my mind that he meant me to pick it up. He was giving me the putt. But seeing that the ball was just a couple of feet from the hole I decided to stop the cross-talk and knock it in.

'I hit the ball practically on the walk and it never got near the hole. I wasn't concentrating and, worse, I had fallen back into my old putting habits. Five weeks ago such a thing would have thrown me completely, I would have three or four putted the rest of the holes. But not now – not with the Trevillion method.'

This was Syd Scott's summing up of the method that beat him: 'It will certainly help the poor putter, it certainly made Adam putt well. This splitting of the hands definitely helps to get over the "twitch"! Sam Snead with his croquet-style proved this. But the real test is, will it help the good putter?'

I was present at the challenge match and I replied, 'Of course it will help the good putter because my method contains every proven principle of good putting. Here, a self-confessed bad putter, Adam Faith, has been transformed into one good enough to beat an ex-Ryder Cup player and on the day Syd Scott did putt well. What pleased me most about Adam's performance was the way he attacked the hole. After his first two putts, both of which he left short, he was always past the hole. On this showing I can't think of any golfer, and I am including the top professionals, who could have beaten Adam. So let's not kid ourselves, what I can do for Adam I can do for a top pro.'

By the completion of the match quite a crowd had gathered at the back of Syd Scott's pro shop. They had all been visibly impressed by what they saw and without exception they made flattering remarks about the method.

Adam Faith summed it all up in these words: 'It was a tremendous gesture on Syd's part to play me; it just shows what a big man he is. Truth is, though, at no time did I think he would beat me. I've so much faith now in the Trevillion method – no pun intended – I expect to hole every putt and I get annoyed if I don't.

'I never lag up, I am really greedy – I want to see them all drop. During the match I knocked a really long one seven feet past, but you can do this sort of thing when you are confident of canning the return as I did. Knocking in putts like I did today was a great feeling and one I certainly never expected to experience. A lot of people said to me after the match that it was a great victory for me, but the truth is that it was a great victory for the Trevillion method.'

It was, indeed, a great victory, a convincing 3 and 1 triumph for Adam Faith, during which he holed three putts of over thirty feet.

Chapter *11*
The Putter Nutter

Scores of converts were turning to the method weekly; even more encouraging, they were winning with it. One of the first to taste success was club golfer Derek Holmes, who scored his first ever Stableford win. Not only that, it was his first win of the season and his first win in division one.

'Thanks a million, Trevillion,' was his first comment. He went on, 'I have followed everything about the Trevillion method since the start. It didn't work immediately and there were times when I could have cheerfully wrapped the club round Trevillion's neck. But I persevered and the putts started dropping.

'I certainly heard some odd comments about the style, for example . . . "Surely that's cheating" and "Do you want to borrow a billiard cue?" Well, my answer to all that is, when the ball's down you can stop counting.'

Holmes's winning round at the Southampton golf club included eight single putts (two thirty-footers); he had a total of twenty-nine putts in all.

John Miller (South Beds. and Royal Cinque Ports) was

another delighted winner. His success came in the Lord Brassey Challenge Cup at Deal. In winning, Miller played six rounds, of which he said, 'I have not putted better for ten years and it's all thanks to the method.' Miller, playing with Graham Clenister, also won the Halford Hewitt Medal Cup with a score of 83 less 5. The competition was played in a howling gale, which made scoring high. His partner, displeased with his putting, turned to the method halfway round with good results and said, after the round, that he putted much better after the change.

The trickle of winners developed into a steady flow. It was now almost impossible to count the number of converts and every bit as difficult to count the number of winners. Every section of the media – newspapers, radio and television – began to take an interest in my putting method and its achievements. I appeared on the television programme *Nationwide*, where they selected the famous British astronomer the late Patrick Moore OBE, a self-confessed bad putter, to put my split-hand putting method to the test. I was given thirty minutes to change Moore into a wizard on the greens.

Under the expert direction of Mark Patterson, the television cameras rolled and the experiment was captured on film. At first it looked as if Moore was a hopeless case as the first putts went well wide of the mark, but eventually the split-hand method found its groove and so did the putts. As one after the other dropped, Patrick exclaimed, 'It works!'

He went on, 'If it can work with me, whose actual handicap is somewhere in the late 70s, it must be good!'

Moore then went off to the golf course with his

golfing companion, TV personality Cliff Michelmore, where he found for the first time in his golfing career that putting was easy – the Trevillion way.

Reaction was swift – over 100 telephone calls were received at the *Golf Illustrated* offices from happy viewers whose one complaint was, 'It didn't last long enough.'

Following this, a BBC national radio interview with Michael Parkinson, who at that time was one of the most respected and powerful voices in the land, provoked a wave of protest and indeed hostility. In fact, even before I had left the building it hit me full blast!

'You're a putter nutter!' snarled a very elderly 'Dickensian'-type gentleman, standing by the doorman. This was the same gentleman who, less than one hour before, when I had entered the building, had greeted me with a very hearty handshake, a smile and the proud boast that he had once played a round of golf with three-times British Open Champion Henry Cotton.

My golfing sin which had evoked such a swift change of character was my claim that I was a better putter from four feet than Billy Casper and Arnold Palmer, two unchallengeable masters of the greens at that time.

'They are both wrist putters,' I pointed out, 'and wrist putters rely on muscle memory. They are not infallible. Furthermore, wrist putters don't last. The small muscles in the wrists break down under constant pressure. Ben Hogan and Sam Snead are proof of that fact.'

'Putter nutter', 'the nutty professor' and even 'maddog Trevillion' were amongst the many names coined to ridicule both myself and my method. Little did I know then that it would take nearly thirty years before it would be the generally accepted fact throughout golf that the delicate muscles of the wrists should be eliminated from the pressure action of the putting stroke.

Chapter 12
The Extended Right Arm

About this time I received a very welcome phone call from Henry Longhurst, the renowned British golf writer, television commentator and former German Amateur Champion, who served for a time as a Member of Parliament when Winston Churchill was Prime Minister.

'I'm sorry, young Paul,' he said, and I detected a note of sadness in his deep, almost royal tone, 'but I feel' – he sighed – 'the golf traditionalists will take a firm, unyielding and united Churchillian stand and never surrender to your method.'

Warming to the battle, he carried on, 'Personally, I believe you are absolutely right. The extended right arm is indeed one of the big secrets of putting. Furthermore, I will show my colours and say as much in my column. Of course the fools will not listen, but don't you give up the fight, young Paul. Your battle, which you have fought bravely and almost single-handed, I believe is lost, but the war is still there to be won.'

I thanked Henry for the call, wished him well and then decided, at least for the time being, to leave the final putt on the method trail to be sunk by the fearless and much beloved Henry Longhurst, who that Sunday, 22 March 1970, wrote at length in the *Sunday Times* about my split-hand putting technique. This is part of what he said:

I am sure as one reasonably can be, both from the advice of an Austrian doctor and my own personal experience which followed, that the extended right arm is one of the secrets of putting. The dreaded twitch, said my doctor friend, comes from the angle of the right elbow (he was the one who added the awful thought that 'violinists get it') and it is a demonstrable fact that even under the most severe pressure you can make a to-and-fro movement with a fully stretched right arm

Henry Longhurst

which you cannot with the normal putting angle. I tried this with such success that rather more than 10 years ago I was moved to declare that with it, if faced with a yard putt to tie for The Open, I could at any rate make some sort of stroke at the ball. I was led astray by the croquet putter and, when that went, I went too.

Even longer ago I had written about some children doing fantastic scores on our rough and ready clock golf course and this prompted a member of Lloyd's to pass on what he described as a 'sensational development of golfing science', based on the performances of an old lady with elastic-sided boots at a fete at Portmarnock. Where he and the local golfers had spent large sums of money on a 12-hole putting course before achieving a score of four under 2's, the old lady with the elastic-sided boots not only went round first time in eight under but was considerably put out on the four occasions when her first putt missed the hole.

After some months of cogitation my friend from Lloyd's hit upon the solution, namely that not only the children I had written about, one of whom would at that time have beaten the better ball of Hogan or Snead with ease – he strode after the ball as he hit it and was ready waiting at the hole side as it fell in – but also the old lady with the elastic-sided boots instinctively picked the club up, as an untaught golfer always does, with the hands wide apart.

'Everything now falls into place,' my correspondent added, 'your children, the old lady, my own vast improvement since I changed over and finally the success of the mallet-putters. Any success achieved by these diabolical weapons is due, in my opinion, not to their shape but simply to the fact that their users hold them with their hands well apart.'

Then, of course, somebody wrote to say that Harold Hilton, Open champion 1892 and 1897, Amateur champion four times, often did it too, thus proving once again that there is nothing new under the golfing sun. I suppose there is nothing for it but to get a pair of elastic-sided boots and the clubs out of the attic, extend the right arm, and start the whole ghastly business all over again.

Chapter 13

Three Wise Men

The Henry Longhurst column in the *Sunday Times* not only silenced the 'putter nutter' taunts, it had many Golf Club secretaries, who had not only banned me from their courses but also insisted I was 'bringing the game of golf into disrepute' (whatever that meant!), phoning me and mumbling that there had been a misunderstanding and that I was welcome back at their clubs. Providing, of course, I did not demonstrate my split-hand putting method on their practice greens for longer than five minutes: 'It might upset some of our members, if they thought you were belittling their prowess with the traditionalist method on the green . . . not the done thing, old boy!'

I always thanked them for the offer, and explained I no longer played eighteen holes of golf but I was more than prepared to pay the green fee for the use of their putting green . . . usually for two hours: 'Sorry, old boy, cannot possibly agree to that,' was always the swift reply. 'More than five minutes would border on an exhibition. Our members would have none of that nonsense.'

I tried to reason with them: 'But your members – those with open minds, of course – might see the merits in my method and benefit from a –'

An interruption invariably came at that juncture in my conversation, 'Merits in your method! Oh, come on now, you're not really serious? Merits! It's bending the rules. It's another version of the Sam Snead croquet style that the United States Golf Association, in its infinite wisdom, banned as illegal.'

I emphasized that my method was nothing like Sam Snead's and it was perfectly legal, but by now the voice on the other end of the line was no longer listening. 'Sorry, I'm very sorry,' it would drone on, 'but golf's a two-handed game – always has been, always will be.'

My parting line was always the same: 'If Henry Long-hurst . . .' – the name always stopped the secretaries in their tracks even when in full verbal flow! – 'If Henry Longhurst came to your club and, as the great man has hinted, used his right arm extended down the putter shaft on your practice putting green, would he be ushered away after a five-minute warm-up? . . . Hello, are you still there? . . .'

A slight cough and then came the reply: 'Henry Longhurst . . . you are talking about one of the pillars of our golfing tradition. Now he would be a special case.'

'And myself,' I would enquire. 'Would I be a "special case" or a "nut case"?'

Another silence and the response invariably: 'I would leave you to decide that, sir!' and the phone would go dead.

Henry Longhurst was soon to be joined by two more

wise old men of golf: British Open Champions and golf-ing legends Max Faulkner and Henry Cotton.

In his excellent book *Play Championship Golf All Your Life*, Max Faulkner wrote:

Recently there has been a great campaign in Britain in favour of a split-handed method of putting publicised by the London artist Paul Trevillion. For short putts I am quite in favour of the two hands being apart. Holding a putter like that does away with wristiness, and if I had been younger I would have had a go at it myself, and I think I would have done well with it, for there is much to be said in its favour. But for short putts only, I fancy.

Henry Cotton said pretty much the same, insisting every golfer should give the Trevillion putting method an extensive trial.

But Henry Cotton was shaking his head gently from side to side when he put his arm round my shoulders and said: 'I'm afraid the answer is no.' He smiled and sighed. 'They do not welcome change in golf. I've suggested to two golfers who were struggling on the greens in last week's British Open to give your method a go; but I'm sorry to say, hard as I tried, they would not listen. Do you know, Paul,' he predicted, 'it will not be an Englishman or an American who will win a major championship with his hands well apart. They are too stubborn, too steeped in tradition. I fancy it will be a European golfer. Possibly one who has gone through all accepted methods of putting, but is still failing on the greens; who, with nowhere else to turn, and in desperation as much as anything else, will turn to your exaggerated hands-apart method and complete the stroke with his shoulders . . . and, do you know, Paul, he will then go on and beat the world's best with it.'

Eighteen years were to pass before Henry Cotton's crystal-gazing prediction proved unerringly correct – Bernhard Langer, with his hands apart, won his first major, the 1985 Masters.

The young German Bernhard Langer had struggled with his first attack of the putting 'yips' at the start of his career when he was eighteen years old. He battled on for some years before changing to the 'cross-handed' method. This proved successful. It appeared he had conquered the 'yips' once and for all.

Unfortunately Langer's stroke began to tighten up. His wrists began to over-react and his putting stroke broke down at the 1988 British Open Championship at Royal Lytham and St Annes, when he five-putted the 17th green on his way to an 80!

It was one of the saddest sights I had witnessed on a putting green. This talented young golfer looked a broken man and the generally accepted opinion in golf was that the German who had tried everything in search of a cure for the putting 'yips' was finished . . . his career over.

Chapter 14
The Reason for Splitting the Hands

In everyday life the left and right hands rarely work as one unit. In general the left hand steadies while the right hand goes to work – knotting a tie; putting your coat on (it's always your right arm you put in first); working with a garden spade; pressing a stubborn toothpaste tube; tying a shoe lace and so on. The moment the left hand has to work with the right, people will say, 'I'm all fingers and thumbs today.' This is because the left hand is hindering, not helping; it is performing an unnatural role and subconsciously your mind rebels against this.

The same goes for putting – on your weekend round you try to get the left and the right hand to work as one unit. You're asking them to adopt an unfamiliar relationship, a relationship which has not been asked of them since the last weekend you played.

What happens? The left hand becomes stubborn, it resists and restricts the working of the right hand at impact, the putt is pulled or pushed to one side of the hole. Even the world's top professionals will remark after a bad round of putting, 'I had no feel in my hands today,'

but this is an inaccurate statement; what they should have said was, 'My left hand was not co-operating.' Your right hand will always react the same, day in and day out. I've never seen or heard of a person attempting to cut a piece of steak remark, 'I just can't keep it on the plate, I have no feel in my hands today.'

The reason the late Orville Moody, winner of the 1969 US Open and a self-confessed bad putter, found success when he adopted the cack-handed grip (right over left) is because when the left hand is in this position it has no function other than to hold the club, the right hand has to do the work.

This is why those elderly gentlemen on bowling greens show no signs of the 'yips'. You can watch them Sunday after Sunday rolling the bowl up with their right hand with no semblance of a shake, and why should there be?

Your right hand is constantly working for you, performing the most difficult tasks, it sees no problems in knocking a putt in the hole. It's just as simple as asking it to undo a button.

A wealthy man I knew, who played a lot of golf and employed a split-handed grip, once told me something I've never forgotten. Taking from his wallet a handful of notes, he said to me, 'Money, no matter how much you've got, is a very precious commodity, and people do not like to make mistakes with such a valuable commodity. This is why they hold the notes with the LEFT HAND and count each one with the RIGHT. The right hand is your BUSINESS HAND; rely on it and it will never let you down.'

Walter Travis, whose many remarkable putting feats gave him a healthy claim to the title 'the greatest putter who ever lived', had this to say on the subject in the book *Great Golfers in the Making*:

I believe that putting should be done always with one hand – with one hand actively at work, that is. The left hand should be used only for the purpose of swinging the clubhead backwards preparatory to making the stroke. When it has done that its work is done, and the right hand should then be the sole master of the situation, the left being merely kept in attachment to it for steadying purposes. WHEN ONLY ONE HAND IS THUS EMPLOYED THE GAIN IN ACCURACY IS VERY GREAT. Two hands at work on a short putt or a long one tend to distraction. When the stroke is being made the grip of the right hand should be firm, but not tight, and after impact the clubhead should be allowed to pass clean through with an easy following stroke. The follow-through should indeed be as long as possible to make it comfortably and with this object in view, at the moment of touching the ball THE GRIP OF THE FINGERS OF THE LEFT HAND SHOULD BE CONSIDERABLY RELAXED SO THAT THE RIGHT HAND MAY GO ON DOING ITS WORK WITHOUT INTERRUPTION.

Which leads on to the question, did Vardon hinder or help? Golf, cricket, baseball, hockey, hurling, lacrosse and ice hockey are all two-handed sports. Of these, golf is the only one in which the hands are overlapped on the grip. Is it right to believe that all these other sports are the ones out of step? Before you make a snap decision I advise you to read on, for I have explained in full the opinion expressed by Mr H. H. Hilton, who played in those historic days when the overlap grip was pioneered.

The big six golfers in those days of gutty balls, wooden cleeks and bumpy greens, were Harry Vardon, J. H. Taylor, James Braid, Alex Herd, Mr H. H. Hilton and Mr John Ball, Jr. Of these Vardon, Taylor and Braid employed the overlapping grip, the other three employed what is known today as the baseball grip, every finger on the club.

It is interesting to recall that the three who used the overlapping grip – Vardon, Taylor and Braid – used a great deal of wrist-work in the stroke. By employing the overlapping grip they ensured the bringing of the hands close together, so allowing both wrists to work in unison.

On the theory of the overlapping grip, Mr Harold H. Hilton – incidentally, the only amateur to win the Open Championship twice and a former editor of *Golf Illustrated* – had this to say: 'Providing you are sufficiently powerful in the hands, try the overlapping grip for it enables the wrists to work together.' Hilton, an extremely small man in stature, standing no more than 5' 6" in height, then added this warning and in doing so underlined why he, a man with average-sized hands, employed the baseball grip. 'I have found that to work the overlapping grip successfully, the golfer must, of necessity, have very long and powerful fingers. For if he has not there is far too much strain placed upon the left hand and wrist and the right hand (three fingers only on the club) does not have a sufficiently firm grip of the club to apply to requisite power.'

With those words, Hilton explained why my split-hand putting technique is the only way to putt. The one thing every golfer agrees on where putting is concerned is that

The two-handed grip

it is a right-handed stroke, so now let's analyse Hilton's remark and check what happens when a golfer mistakenly putts with the overlap grip:

1. He considerably weakens the master right hand.
2. Both wrists have to work in unison.
3. A simple one-handed strike is turned into a complicated two-handed action.

THE TREVILLION METHOD

With my split-handed putting method, the left hand serves but one purpose, it anchors the club position. Now the right hand is free to do its job – UNHINDERED by the left. The stroke now becomes one of simplicity; the right hand, with all fingers on the club, assumes complete authority over the striking action.

I can think of no other sport where fellow professionals check each other's grip – which, to my way of thinking, leads me to believe that over-emphasis on the Vardon grip has HINDERED as much as it has helped golf, especially PUTTING.

THE PENCIL PUTT TEST

When putting, the secret is to take the putter straight back and through – an extremely difficult thing to do if you adopt the Vardon overlap grip. You can prove this for yourself by holding a pencil in your normal putting grip and then drawing a line. It will, I assure you, be far from straight. Now hold the pencil in just your right

The Vardon Grip

hand (providing you are right-handed) and draw another line under the one which you have just completed. You will, I promise, be surprised just how much straighter the second line is.

Chapter 15

The Truth About the Cross-Hand Putting Method

When a golfer as technically correct as South African Gary Player openly admits that he has been using the wrong putting grip since he started golf, the time has come when every deep-thinking golfer must seriously consider if he is using the correct grip.

At the time of writing, Player, desperately seeking a cure, was experimenting with the cross-handed putting grip, insisting that it was not a panic measure but the result of a lot of thought. For Player's information I can prove, without fear of contradiction, that this will lead to only a temporary cure. Player is metaphorically driving down a one-way street in the wrong direction – he will eventually have to stop, reverse and start again.

In that excellent book *Golf's Winning Stroke: Putting* we find the following:

The cross-handed putting grip began to enjoy a considerable vogue about 1965. Fred Haas, Jr, the veteran New Orleans professional who became the United States Seniors Champion in 1965, had been using the technique for several years. It was

Johnny Pott

Orville Moody

subsequently adopted by such successful pros as Johnny Pott, Wes Ellis, Jr, Jim Ferree, Peter Alliss and among the ladies, Marilyn Smith. As its name implies, the essential feature of this grip is that the hands are crossed. There are minor variations of this grip. Ellis describes his own – 'My grip is the interlocking with the little finger of my left hand twining round the fore-finger of my right hand. I putt right-handed, the back of my left hand and the palm of my right hand face towards the hole. My thumbs are directly on top of the shaft. The face of the putter remains square to the line for a longer time without any special effort on my part to keep it square.'

Johnny Pott went so far as to have a specially manufactured putter grip with a flat top. This enabled him to place both thumbs on the flat surface and for him it helped considerably. As it was, both Ellis and Pott proved better than average putters with the cross-handed method.

In 1969 Orville Moody exploded on to the golf scene when he won the US Open putting cross-handed. Said Orville at the time:

'The reason I switched was because I developed a case of the "yips". I'd yip one left of the hole and then on the next putt, I'd try not to do that and I'd leave it on the other side. I putted so poorly I just had to do something.'

Orville described his technique thus – 'I placed the right hand up high on the grip. The left hand is placed directly below the right, but with all my fingers on the shaft – no overlapping.' (This is an improvement on the Pott–Ellis method, where overlapping and interlocking was employed.) 'Putting has always been a right-handed action for me and this method helps me to keep the ball on line. A one-piece arm motion ensures that the wrists remain firm.'

The magazine *Golf Monthly*'s renowned contributor Mr X has this to say on the cross-handed grip:

It works because it keeps the shoulders level at address, while the orthodox putting grip tends to raise the left shoulder and lower the right. But when the left shoulder is higher than the right at address and there is any shoulder movement during the putt then the left shoulder tends to turn away from the line, causing the putt to be cut.

From what I have said readers will note that the main advantages for the cross-handed method of putting are:

(a) It keeps the shoulders level at address.
(b) It allows the right hand to execute the stroke.
(c) There is a much firmer anchor point as the left hand is nearer the putter blade.
(d) When the shoulders are level at address then the left shoulder can RISE (during the putting action) without turning.

JORDAN SPIETH

Major winner Jordan Spieth employs the cross-handed method when putting. Spieth sinks more than his share of long putts. But he also misses many hole-able short putts.

I believe that, like me, Michelangelo would question the left hand that appears to guide the putter face to the hole.

Chapter 16
Feel

Feel is the biggest misconception in putting. It's non-sense to say, and many great putters do, that you must hold the club no tighter than when feeling your own pulse.

To say you must feel the grip in your hand for 'touch' when putting, I repeat, is a total *misconception*.

You can check this out for yourself when building with cards, coins or whatever; the higher you get, the more delicately you try to place the next one on top and, eventually, it's your shaking, unsteady hand that topples the lot.

Ninety per cent of golfers take the wrists out of the putting action, but then they subconsciously reintroduce them when they strive for feel when gripping the club.

You should instead hold your putter tightly enough to ensure you feel the putter head strike the ball. The same way an artist only feels the pencil point on the paper. He is totally unaware of holding the pencil.

The truth is, it's impossible to pull a pencil from the finger and thumb of an artist, so strong and positive is

Renoir

his grip when drawing. In short the grip is *tight* but never *tense*.

Don't take my word for it. The great French master Renoir, helpless in his old age, crippled with arthritis and twisted joints, considered himself a lucky man because he was able to paint in his bath chair with the brush bound tightly to his wrist with rolls of sticking tape. Renoir called it 'putting on his thumb'. The Renoir brush strokes transferred to canvas in this manner seemed to gain in youth and energy.

Renoir accepted that he could no longer sculpt, but by directing the hands of two young artists by means of a long stick strapped to his wrist, like a magic wand, he

Bernhard Langer

conjured up a massive sculpture of a young goddess of breathtaking beauty.

The struggle of the crippled artist is one of the heroic legends of art.

Today Bernhard Langer grips the club with his left hand well down the shaft, then uses his right hand to strap the putter to his left arm. Then, like Renoir, he draws a straight line to the hole and invariably the putt drops in.

Chapter 17

Straight Back – Straight Through

On short putts, the putter blade must be taken *straight back* and *straight through* to the hole.

For those who say the putter blade must be taken back slightly *inside* the line then straightened up again in line with the hole on impact with the ball, I say think again.

To deliberately take the putter blade off line once you have painstakingly lined it up is madness. You are relying on muscle memory to straighten it up again and nobody is that good. More short putts are missed in this manner than in any other way.

Secondly, the blade must travel low to the ground back and through the stroke to ensure impact on the centre of the ball. This produces a true roll. The ball is round; if struck correctly in this manner the ball will hug the ground and keep its line.

If the blade lifts when you make contact with the ball on your follow-through, you will impart too much over-spin and the ball will roll with less control.

If you lift the blade on the backswing, chances are you

will make contact with the ball with a downwards strike and impart excess backspin and the ball will finish short of the hole.

Chapter 18
Never Be Short

No golfer has suffered more on the greens than the 'voice of golf', Peter Alliss, which is why I have never met anyone who speaks with more authority or sense on the art of getting the ball into the hole.

It was Alliss who told me that, as long as I lived, I would never find a hole that would come up and meet the ball – the ball must go to the hole. Alliss also believed, and rightly so, that the golfer who misses his putts by going past the hole is an infinitely better putter than the player who misses his by always being short.

The player who is always finishing six inches short very seldom three-putts, but then he will hardly, if ever, one-putt. Whereas the player who, when he misses, is always going past the hole gets a great number of single putts. Yes, he may also get a couple of threes, but if you don't get your share of one-putts you are not going to win a Championship.

The greatest pressure-putter in the history of golf was undoubtedly Arnold Palmer.

Arnold thought nothing of charging the first putt four

feet past the hole. The return, he considered, was a simple tap-in.

I think American Doug Ford, winner of the Masters and a great pressure-putter, summed it up best when he said: 'I was never short with my first, second, third, fourth or fifth putt!'

So there you have it. Be brave . . . go for the hole and knock it in. There is no other way to win a Championship.

Chapter 19
The Putting Greats

I have spent almost half a century researching and analysing the great putters who have dominated Championship golf. My special heroes all come from a similar mould, preach pretty much the same techniques and sank most of those all-important four-footers.

If you study my method you will find it contains all the proven principles that these great men moulded into their Championship-winning putting stroke.

HARRY VARDON – STOOPED TO CONQUER

All the early golfing greats – Harry Vardon, Walter J. Travis, Walter Hagen, Gene Sarazen – got well down to their work. They were all confirmed crouchers over the ball.

The centre or axis of the putting stroke is the top of the spine between the shoulder blades.

In a crouched position using this axis, the shoulders, arms and hands move in a line parallel to the green.

If anyone knows of a better human support for a

Harry Vardon

pendulum, he should immediately inform the medical council.

SAM SNEAD — THE SIDE SADDLE

Slamming Sam Snead was a dynamic wrist putter. He had to be, to have won over 100 tournaments.

Then in 1966 at the Firestone Club in Akron, Ohio, Sam set up short birdie putts on the first nine holes and missed the lot.

On the 10th hole Sam straddled the line and, croquet-style, rattled the putts in.

The US Golf Association banned the stance as illegal.

Sam changed to side saddle. Hinging the club at the

top of the grip, Sam used the shoulder and the whole arm, with the wrist of the moving arm taken out of the stroke.

Sam cleaned up on the Seniors tour.

Sam Snead

SIR BOB CHARLES – THE PENDULUM

Sir Bob Charles is still the finest left-handed putter in the game.

Charles favours the square method of putting. Hands parallel to each other, shoulders, hips, feet in line with the hole. Putter blade in line with the hole.

Charles takes the putter straight back and straight through, his shoulders moving in a vertical plane, creating the perfect pendulum action.

Bob Charles

Every inch you raise the head above the horizontal tilts the axis of the swing and introduces inaccuracies.

ARNOLD PALMER — POWER PUTTER

The most confident, positive and attacking putter of my time was Arnold Palmer.

He thought nothing of banging the ball four feet past. The return distance was a tap-in.

Most short putts are missed due to the failure to follow through. This is caused by fear of being too firm.

Yet firmness is demanded even in the shortest of strokes.

There are those who say the follow-through has no

Arnold Palmer

effect whatsoever on what happens to the ball once it has left the club face.

Nonsense – this is where the confidence of the golfer is exposed.

A confident follow-through makes the putt. It's a clear indication of what went on before the ball left the club face.

You must take the putter face to the hole.

JACK NICKLAUS – FREEZE FRAME

Jack Nicklaus bends low over the ball in a crouched position.

Jack holds his putter almost vertical at address to

Jack Nicklaus

ensure he swings the club pendulum-like, with the putter face on line to the hole throughout the stroke.

Jack holds his breath, as if he's frozen in ice throughout the stroke. It allows his body to remain still and only his arms to make the stroke.

Nobody in the history of golf has played the pressure putts better.

LEE TREVINO — TEN-FINGER GRIP

The name of the game is getting the ball in the hole and no golfer has done it better than Lee Trevino.

I remember Lee telling me he placed all ten fingers on the grip by sliding his right hand down the grip a fraction. This gave him the feeling of having more control with his right hand. Then, by placing both of his thumbs

Lee Trevino

pointing straight down the shaft, he had both palms facing and this kept the wrists out of action as much as possible.

With the hands in this position Lee believed he prevented pushing or pulling a putt and he was dead right.

Trevino never faces a pressure putt, because with his method there is no pressure.

SAM TORRANCE — BROOM HANDLE

Sam Torrance popularized the Broom Handle technique, but the critics say putting should be about feel and the Broom Handle is nothing more than a mechanical action. Nonsense. Short putts have nothing to do with feel. It's about swinging the club like a pendulum.

Sam Torrance

Torrance hinges the club at his chin. The left hand and arm have no place in the stroke, except to anchor the top of the handle to the chin.

The right hand holds the club like a pencil and the putter blade is directed along the line of the putt by the whole of the right arm. This method is now illegal.

BERNHARD LANGER – THE MECHANIC

The Langer method is technically the Broom Handle stroke in miniature.

Langer grips the club with his left hand then uses his right hand to clamp the putter to his left arm. The clamp prevents the left wrist from breaking down.

Bernhard Langer

As with the Broom Handle, the action requires a large shoulder movement for even the shortest putt.

In short, it's a small stroke controlled by the big muscles.

Chapter 20

The Perfect Putting Method

I will now talk you through the thinking behind what I call my *one-putt knock-in*.

1. The Putting Stance

As Sugar Ray Robinson said, the width your feet are apart with your natural walking stride is the perfect platform for your body weight. So that is your putting stance. Check it out: drop a ball on the floor and walk up to it. Stop and now bend your knees and you are as solid and as steady as a rock.

No body or head movement throughout the arms and club-putting stroke.

2. The Putting Crouch

I tilt from the waist and ensure my shoulders are parallel to the ground. The centre or axis of the putting stroke is the top of the spine between the shoulder blades. You could place a tray across my back and balance a drinking-glass on top and the liquid inside the glass would be perfectly level.

3. The Soling of the Putter

I have the sole of my putter perfectly level with the ground. I start my putting stroke by lifting it slightly, to ensure I do not catch the grass on the backswing and follow-through.

4. Eyes Over the Ball

My eyes are directly over the ball. You can check this out by dropping a ball from the bridge of your nose. It should land on the ball below.

5. Alignment to the Hole – The Square Method

With all short putts the ball must be hit firmly enough to eliminate any borrow along a straight line to the hole.

Having decided on your line to the hole, your putter club-face and body must be positioned along this line square to the hole. This is known as 'The Square Method'. Your feet, ankles, knees, hips and shoulders are in line with the hole.

6. Grip Pressure

My grip is tight, just like I hold a pencil; but it is never *tense*. I repeat, *never tense*. Forget 'feel' for the short putt. The ball is too close to the hole for 'feel' to play any part.

Don't just take my word for it, check it out. Palmer aside, the two greatest pressure-putters of all time, Jack Nicklaus and Lee Trevino, putt with their gloves on. Now, if you wanted maximum 'feel', wouldn't it be smart to putt with the glove off?

So, I repeat, forget 'feel' when it comes to the short putt.

7. The Pendulum Stroke

Both my arms hang naturally from the shoulders with both palms of my hands facing each other and perfectly level with each other. Because I want to take my right palm to the hole pendulum-fashion, I take my left hand out of the stroke by placing it at the top of the grip. Using my right shoulder I take the club straight back and through.

8. The Strike

As a mental image I imagine the ball is asleep. I give it a
hard whack, its eyes open . . . it sees the hole and it dives
in. The putt's history!

9. The Follow-Through

A confident follow-through sinks the putt. It's a clear indication of what went on before you struck the ball. You must take the putter face to the hole.

Chapter 21

Why Four Feet?

The question I'm asked most is 'why four feet?'

Firstly, from that distance the borrow doesn't decide the fate of the putt. If the ball is hit hard enough it will take out any borrow even on a fast green with a downhill left-to-right putt. Secondly, I'll take you back to Muirfield, the year is 1972 and it's the 17th hole of the final round of the British Open. Lee Trevino is in the rough and Tony Jacklin is on the green. Trevino from the rough chips in and from four feet Jacklin three-putts!

Trevino won the 1972 British Open and Jacklin, who up to that time could putt the eyes out of a squirrel, was never a serious contender for the Major Championships again.

There are hundreds of great putters – too many for me to mention – who have been broken and destroyed from the four-foot area. They know they shouldn't miss, but they do. That is why my split-hand method, fifty years on, is now becoming fashionable.

Nevertheless, there are still many traditionalists and 'doubting Thomases' who challenge my method . . . they call it a 'gimmick'.

In the same way Johnny 'Tarzan' Weissmuller, who was never beaten in over 100 swimming races and who won a bucketful of Olympic Golds with his revolutionary front-crawl whiplash leg action – he used each leg as a whip and his feet as a lash, propelling himself forward with unbelievable power – was told his method was a 'gimmick'.

In the 1968 Olympics, Bob Fosbury revolutionized the High Jump with his backward leap . . . They called his method a 'gimmick'.

In the early 1970s the USA's Jimmy Connors introduced the two-handed backhand return. They laughed and said 'it's fine for the ladies like Chris Evert because they are the weaker sex.'

Once again they called it a 'gimmick'.

I will tell you the definition of a 'gimmick'. It's something you wished you had thought of first. Which is so sad, especially when I think back to 1968.

The place was my house. It was there that I showed Peter Alliss, TV's Mr Golf, my putting method.

A ball was placed on the carpet four feet from the leg of a chair and, with Alliss watching, I hit that chair leg with six consecutive putts using my split-hand method.

Alliss adopted the method and repeated the feat, but with a difference. Each of his strikes was so true that the ball rolled back to him, whereas the majority of mine had bounced off at different angles.

Three days later, I saw Peter on the Stoke Poges practice putting green. I asked him if he was experimenting with my method. He gave a practical answer . . . he separated his grip and knocked in three four-footers.

'Are you going to use it in the tournament?' I asked.

He shook his head. 'I have a tough enough job explaining how I miss with the conventional method. I'd be lost for words using your method.'

Alliss finished second in the tournament to Clive Clark, but had he used my method he would have won. He missed four putts of under four feet.

Alliss was the one man I feared in those days. He was a better putter with my method than Bernhard Langer.

I have no doubts that if Peter Alliss had adopted my method he would have won a lot of majors. He was that good a golfer.

The first golfer to have the moral courage to adopt my method to improve his putting when he is already a good putter will be perfection on the greens.

I'm not a golfer, I don't profess to having much of a game, but I am an artist who can draw a straight line on a green . . . and, from four feet, I can beat any golfer in the world.

Acknowledgements

Sincere thanks to Peter Willis, who, as deputy editor of *Golf Illustrated* magazine in the sixties, was the first to break the story of my split-hand Pencil Grip putting theories, and who over the last fifty years has never wavered in his belief that splitting the hands on the putter and striking the ball with the master hand was the surest way to hole tournament-winning putts. Opposition and ridicule to my theories in those early days was rife, but Peter and *Golf Illustrated* editor Tom Scott never wavered in their belief that I had come up with a groundbreaking putting method that was newsworthy.

Without them, the split-hand Pencil Grip revolution would never have taken off, and many golfers today would still be suffering the agonies of missing a short putt in ignorance of a proven putting method that can defeat this eternal golfing nightmare.